DARE TO DREAM
LEADER GUIDE

Dare to Dream
Series

Dare to Dream:
Creating a God-Sized Mission Statement for Your Life
978-1-4267-7577-2

Dare to Dream
DVD
978-1-4267-7578-9

Dare to Dream
Leader Guide
978-1-4267-7579-6

Dare to Dream
Youth Book
978-1-4267-7580-2

Dare to Dream
Youth DVD
978-1-4267-7582-6

Dare to Dream
Children's Leader Guide
978-1-4267-7581-9

Dare to Dream
Preview Book
978-1-4267-7583-3

MIKE SLAUGHTER

DARE TO DREAM

CREATING A GOD-SIZED MISSION STATEMENT FOR YOUR LIFE

LEADER GUIDE
BY MARTHA BETTIS GEE

Abingdon Press
Nashville

Mike Slaughter
Dare to Dream: Creating a God-Sized Mission Statement for Your Life

Leader Guide by Martha Bettis Gee

This book is printed on acid-free, elemental chlorine-free paper.

Library of Congress Cataloging-in-Publication applied for.
ISBN 978-1-4267-7579-6

13 14 15 16 17 18 19 20 21 22—10 9 8 7 6 5 4 3 2 1

MANUFACTURED IN THE UNITED STATES OF AMERICA

CONTENTS

To the Leader

Welcome! In this study, you have the opportunity to help a group of learners as they seek to create a life mission statement that can put flesh on a God-dream worth living for.

This study was written with three purposes in mind. First, the author, Mike Slaughter, wants to wake up those in the study to the God-dream inside. Second, he wants to help participants to develop a life mission statement. This he distinguishes from life goals, which he says may change by season or circumstance while a life mission statement never changes. Third, he wants to challenge participants to commit fully to the God-directed life mission they create.

These purposes distinguish this study from some other studies in which participants are mostly seeking to gain knowledge. It is even different from studies in which participants are seeking to deepen their faith. To be sure, participants who fully commit to this study will gain knowledge and deepen their faith, but they may also find themselves moved to reorient their lives around a mission, aligning their lives with God's purpose for a world in which healing and wholeness prevail.

As the leader, you can best help participants if you first work through the chapters and draft your own life mission statement. Then, as you lead the group, you may find yourself revising your draft in the light of interactions with other persons committed to the process. Scripture tells us that where two or three are gathered together, we can be assured of the presence of the Holy Spirit working in and through all those gathered. As you prepare to lead, pray for that presence and expect that you will experience it.

This six-session study makes use of the following components:

- Mike Slaughter's book *Dare to Dream*;
- a DVD in which Slaughter, using stories and Scripture, presents and expands upon key points from the book; and
- this leader guide.

Participants in the study may also find it useful to have a journal in which to record notes and do homework assignments between the sessions. The journal can be as simple as a notebook, or it may be a file on an electronic device such as a tablet. (Note that space is also provided in the *Dare to Dream* book for taking notes and working on a life mission statement.) Encourage participants to bring the journal to group sessions, along with a Bible.

Also note that while this leader guide covers the six core chapters of the *Dare to Dream* book, remember to read Mike Slaughter's prologue and epilogue, and encourage participants to do the same. Feel free to discuss the prologue during Session 1 and the epilogue during Session 6.

Congregations seeking a churchwide emphasis may also want to use these additional components in the program, all based on Mike Slaughter's book *Dare to Dream*:

- a youth book written by Jenny Youngman,
- a youth DVD featuring Nick Cunningham, and
- a children's leader guide for older and younger children with reproducible handouts, written by Sally Hoelscher.

Using This Guide with Your Group

Because no two groups are alike, this guide has been designed to give you flexibility and choice in tailoring the sessions for your group. The session format is listed below. You may choose any or all of the activities, adapting them as you wish to meet the schedule and needs of your particular group.

You may find that your session time is too short to do all the activities, in which case you'll want to select ahead of time which activities the group will do, for how long, and in what order.

In some sessions, the session format is adapted in order to best fit the content of the chapter. For example, in some cases Bible study and study of the book blend seamlessly together, and so the format is arranged to best fit that reality.

For some sessions, there are activities that require special preparation. In that case, the leader is alerted to those requirements at the beginning of the session plan.

Session Format

Planning the Session
    Session Goals
    Special Preparation (if needed)
    Biblical Foundation

Getting Started
    Opening Prayer
    Opening Activity

Learning Together
    Video Study and Discussion
    Bible Study and Discussion
    Book Study and Discussion
    Building a Life Mission Statement

Wrapping Up
  Closing Activity
  Closing Prayer

Helpful Hints

Preparing for the Session

- Pray for the leading of the Holy Spirit as you prepare for the study. Pray for discernment for yourself and for each member of the study group;
- As mentioned above, work through the study book (*Dare to Dream*) and use the process to develop a draft of your own life mission statement in advance of the study;
- Before each session, familiarize yourself with the book chapter content. Read the chapter again and watch the video segment;
- Choose the session elements you will use during the group session, including the specific discussion questions you plan to cover. Be prepared, however, to adjust the session as group members interact and as questions arise. Prepare carefully, but allow space for the Holy Spirit to move in and through the material, the group members, and you as facilitator;
- Secure a TV and DVD player in advance;
- Prepare the meeting space so that it will enhance the learning process. Ideally, group members should be seated around a table or in a circle so that all can see one another. Movable chairs are best because the group will sometimes be forming pairs or small groups for discussion;
- Bring a supply of Bibles for those who forget to bring their own. Having a variety of translations is helpful;
- Encourage participants to bring journals along with their Bibles. Make paper and pens or pencils available;
- For most sessions you will also need a chalkboard and chalk, a white board and markers, or an easel with paper and markers.

Shaping the Learning Environment
- Begin and end on time;
- Create a climate of openness, encouraging group members to participate as they feel comfortable. Remember that some persons will jump right in with answers and comments, while others need time to process what is being discussed;
- If you notice that some group members never seem able to enter the conversation, ask if they have thoughts to share. Give everyone a chance to talk, but keep the conversation moving. Intervene where necessary to prevent a few individuals from doing all the talking;
- Communicate the importance of group discussions and group exercises;
- If no one answers at first during discussions, do not be afraid of silence. Count silently to ten; then say something such as "Would anyone like to go first?" If no one responds, venture an answer yourself and ask for comments;
- Model openness as you share with the group. Group members will follow your example. If you limit your sharing to a surface level, others will follow suit;
- Encourage multiple answers or responses before moving on;
- Ask, "Why?" or "Why do you believe that?" or "Can you say more about that?" to help continue a discussion and give it greater depth;
- Affirm others' responses with comments such as "Great," "Thanks," or "Good insight"—especially if this is the first time someone has spoken during the group session;
- Monitor your own contributions. If you are doing most of the talking, back off so that you do not train the group to listen rather than speak up;
- Remember that you do not have all the answers. Your job is to keep the discussion going and encourage participation;

Managing the Session

- Honor the time schedule. If a session is running longer than expected, get consensus from the group before continuing beyond the original ending time;
- Involve group members in various aspects of the session such as playing the DVD, saying prayers, and reading the Scripture;
- Note that the session guides sometimes call for breaking into smaller teams. This gives everyone a chance to speak and participate fully. Mix up the teams; don't let the same people pair up on every activity;
- Because many activities call for personal sharing, confidentiality is essential. Group members should never pass along stories that have been shared in the group. Remind the group members at each session: confidentiality is crucial to the success of this study.

1. DREAMING THE DREAM

Planning the Session

Session Goals

As a result of conversations and activities connected with this session, group members should begin to:

- explore the differences between a God-dream and more self-directed desires and plans;
- examine dreams and waking visions as a way God has of getting our attention;
- reflect on dreams and visions as "thin places" where heaven and earth connect;
- identify three people they admire, and answer questions about the qualities those people exemplify, the steps they took to nurture those qualities, why those qualities are important, and the difference those qualities could make in participants' lives; and
- take the first steps toward developing a life mission statement.

Biblical Foundation

When Jacob woke from his sleep, he thought to himself, The LORD is definitely in this place, but I didn't know it. He was terrified and thought, This sacred place is awesome. It's none other than God's house and the entrance to heaven.

(Genesis 28:16-17)

Getting Started

Opening Prayer

God, you have created us for so much more. Reveal to us how to live life in the abundance of your empowering Spirit. May we say with Jesus when our days on this earth are done, "I have glorified you on earth by finishing the work you gave me to do." Amen.

Opening Activity

As group members arrive, welcome them to the study. If there is someone who did not bring a notebook or an electronic device such as a tablet or laptop for journaling, provide a notebook or paper and pen or pencil. If group members are not familiar with one another, provide nametags.

Gather together. On a sheet of paper or a board, print the following open-ended prompt:

Someday I'm going to...

Invite group members to give responses to the statement, and jot those responses on the sheet. Point out that in the prologue to the study book, the author completes the statement in a somewhat surprising way. What does he say? Invite group members to respond to the observation that "someday" is the enemy to the gift of today.

Ask group members to look over the responses listed on the sheet. In what ways might these responses be the enemy of the gift of today? Based on what the author says, what is the difference between daydreaming and God-dreaming?   P. 9

Invite a volunteer to read aloud the final paragraph of the   P 10
book's prologue, where the author names the three purposes he had in mind when writing the book. On another sheet, list those three purposes. In order to keep the purposes in mind during the rest of the study, tell the group that you will continue to post them for the next five sessions. Encourage group members to keep in mind their "someday" responses, and those of others, as they begin to explore what it means to live God's dream.

Learning Together

Video Study and Discussion

Briefly introduce Mike Slaughter, the book author and video presenter. Information about him can be found on the back of the book and DVD package. If group members have smartphones, also direct them to http://ginghamsburg.org/bring/our-pastors/mike-slaughter for a profile of Slaughter. The homepage of the Ginghamsburg church, http://ginghamsburg.org, can give participants more information about the church he serves.

To set the stage for the video, invite group members to tell in a sentence or two what they know about the Wright brothers. Tell them that throughout these videos, the experiences and dreams of these innovators will provide a context for the study. Then show the first video.

Following the video, invite the group to discuss the following:

- In the video, Mike Slaughter refers to the BHAG (Big Hairy Audacious God-Purpose), a concept based on the work of Stanford University business professor Jim Collins.[1] What is a BHAG? How does Slaughter say we can know our BHAG when we see it?

- What are "thin places" in Celtic spirituality? In what ways does Slaughter believe God uses dreams as thin places?
- Mike Slaughter journals about his dreams and believes that God speaks to him through the dreams. Discuss the example of his dream about the child in the road. What does he believe God was saying to him in that dream? What was God saying to B.W. Day in his "waking dream," the vision about Ginghamsburg?

Form pairs and ask group members to talk together about dreams they have had that seemed significant. Invite them to respond to Slaughter's belief that God can speak through dreams. Has this been their experience? If so, what specific messages do they believe they have received from God? In the large group, invite volunteers to describe briefly their experiences of dreaming and of waking experiences of insight.

Bible Study and Discussion

Slaughter uses the story of Jacob in Genesis 28 as the biblical foundation for this session. Ask volunteers to tell what they remember about Jacob and briefly review what the study book and the video segment have to say about the circumstances that brought Jacob to Bethel. Then ask a volunteer to read aloud Genesis 28:1-17. Discuss the following:

- How would you describe Jacob in one or two words? If you were choosing a person to carry on God's covenant to make a people as numerous as the dust of the earth, what personal characteristics would that person have? Did Jacob meet those criteria?
- Jacob encountered God on the staircase connecting heaven and earth. Where have you encountered God? What "thin places" can you identify? If you have not had that experience, are there ways to make yourself more alert when God may be trying to get your attention?

- Have you ever experienced a sense of restlessness that would not be quieted? What was the result of that restlessness? Was it an occasion of change, or did you ignore or stifle the feeling and continue with life as usual? What does the author mean by "living the dream"?

The author observes that throughout Scripture, God uses dreams and visions to get people's attention. Invite participants to form pairs with someone other than the persons they were paired with before. Ask one person in each pair to read Job 33:14-18 and the other to read Acts 9:10-11; then discuss the following with their partner:

- Mike Slaughter notes that we may miss God's voice because it can be drowned out by the busyness, the concerns, and the crises of our daily lives. But when we are asleep, God can often speak to us in ways that get our full attention. When have you sensed a warning about a temptation or something harmful in a dream? If you have not experienced this, can you recall a dream that might have represented such a warning?
- Slaughter also describes what he calls a waking vision, such as the vision Ananias had in Acts 9. Talk about a time when a person popped into your thoughts, seemingly at random. What action, if any, did you take?
- Slaughter identifies the Holy Spirit as the Companion, as in John 14:16-19. He identifies the Holy Spirit as the Presence perhaps speaking through dreams and waking visions. When have you experienced the nudging of the Companion? When, if ever, have you experienced the Spirit calling you in unnerving or unsettling ways?

Book Study and Discussion
Review with the group what the author calls the BHAG. Ask participants to name the three criteria Slaughter uses to

discriminate our God-purpose from our own self-centered plans or desires. List these criteria for the group to see.

Call attention to what Mike Slaughter says about his own experiences over his lifetime of answering the childhood question, "What do you want to be when you grow up?" Invite group members to create a page in their journals with that question at the top. Down the side of the page, have them put the words *childhood, adolescence, young adulthood, middle age*, and *older adulthood*.

Then ask them to write how they answered that question at each life stage they have experienced. In small groups ask participants to share their responses. Come together in the large group to discuss the following:

- Mike Slaughter tells how he fell into retail management as a college major. Have you ever had a similar experience regarding vocational choice, college plans, or other important life events? Tell about that experience.
- Which of those choices have led to aspects of your life that you are now reluctant to change? Why?
- What routines of daily living have created ruts in your life? Which of those ruts really represent significant pathways that shape your life in positive ways, and which are ruts that direct you in rigid directions that need redirection?

Building Your Life Mission Statement: Part 1

At the end of Chapter 1, Mike Slaughter invites readers to begin the process of developing a life mission statement by identifying three people they admire and answering three questions about each of them.

- What are the greatest qualities that you think these people exemplify?
- What steps have these people taken to nurture the qualities?

- Why are the qualities important to you? How would your life be different if you lived more effectively into these qualities?

Slaughter discusses one of his choices, Bono of the rock group U2, and the BHAG Bono has identified. Slaughter makes the point that, like the Wright brothers whose day job was running a bicycle shop, Bono's BHAG is not his day job. His passion, and ultimately his life, is about service and not success. Discuss the following:

- How do you define success in your own life? If it is tied to your career, do you feel you have achieved success, and if so, how do you measure it? By achieving a certain position or salary? If it is tied to family life, what makes your family a success?
- Mike Slaughter observes that life is not about chasing money; it is about fulfilling a mission. How do you think our culture defines success?
- What forces are at play in our consumer culture that shape that definition?
- Would your definition of success meet the test of a God-purpose?

Call the group's attention to the questions at the end of book Chapter 1, under "Building Your Life Mission Statement: Part 1." Ask them to pause for a time of silent prayer, seeking discernment in identifying three people they admire.

Invite group members to list the three people in their book or journal and then to answer the first question about all three people, listing the greatest qualities they exemplify. After allowing a few minutes for group members to work individually on the question, ask a volunteer or two to name one of the persons he or she chose and some of the qualities he or she identified.

Wrapping Up

Closing Activity

Call attention again to the sheet on which you recorded group members' responses to the open-ended prompt, "Someday, I'm going to..." Mike Slaughter observes that his job is to remind his congregants that they are going to die. Ask the group to consider in silence those responses in the light of the reality of death. Ask them to reflect on the following:

- Which of the things I look forward to doing someday meet the test of fulfilling a God-purpose?
- If I die sooner rather than later, what will I have accomplished?

Encourage group members to finish answering the questions before the next session about the three people they admire. Also invite group members to place their books or journals next to their beds each night before going to sleep. Ask them to jot down any dreams they have immediately upon waking. In the next few days, ask them to reflect on any dream that seems significant, asking God to point the way toward discernment of any messages that a dream may have.

Participants may also try to identify a time or location during the week that seems to represent a "thin place" between heaven and earth. It might be a porch or quiet room where they can read Scripture and meditate, or a time such as early morning or late evening when they can make themselves available to the stirrings of the Holy Spirit. Remind them that ideally this is not merely a book study; it is process designed to help open them up to God's purpose for their lives.

Closing Prayer

Holy One, we yearn for the experience of encountering you on holy ground. Make us receptive to your Holy Spirit and sensitive to your purpose for our lives. For in Jesus' name we pray. Amen.

2. Discovering Your Birthright

Planning the Session

Session Goals

As a result of conversations and activities connected with this session, group members should begin to:

- distinguish the difference between identity and birthright, and identify how to find their birthright;
- determine and claim what is at the "top of the ladder" in their own lives; and
- identify needs and gifts in preparation for developing a life mission statement.

Special Preparation

You will need drawing or copy paper and fine-lined black markers for participants, as well as copies of the front page and ad sections of a local newspaper, an Internet news site, or a news magazine such as *Time*.

"*If*"

Biblical Foundation

After Jacob got up early in the morning, he took the stone he had put near his head, set it up as a sacred pillar, and poured oil on the top of it. . . . Jacob made a solemn promise: "If God is with me and protects me on this trip I'm taking, and gives me bread to eat and clothes to wear, and I return safely to my father's household, then the LORD will be my God. This stone that I've set up as a sacred pillar will be God's house, and of everything you give me I will give a tenth back."

(Genesis 28:18, 20-22)

Getting Started

Opening Prayer

Holy God, guide us this day as we seek to discern the God-dream inside each of us. Help us to see how our own God-dream will honor you, bless others in real ways, and bring us joy. In the name of Jesus Christ your Son. Amen.

Opening Activity

As group members arrive, invite them to form groups of two or three to discuss their answers to the questions posed in the last session. Each person should first name one of the three persons he or she admires, then the qualities that person exemplifies and how that person nurtured those qualities. If someone does not know how the qualities were nurtured, discuss how the nurturing might have taken place. Could it have been through the influence of a parent or adult mentor? Through a community of faith? As a result of some experience or encounter? Encourage group members to share with one another why the named qualities are important to them.

In the large group, invite each smaller group to report the qualities they identified, and list these on a sheet for the group to see. If a quality is named more than once, indicate it by

Why?

putting a check mark next to the named quality. Then discuss how each quality might make a difference in a person's life. Encourage group members to keep in mind the qualities they admire and aspire to themselves as they continue to reflect on developing a life mission statement.

Remind group members that they may want to keep a journal handy at their bedside for jotting down dreams. Invite any volunteers who tried this during the past week to describe the experience of recording dreams and any insights that seemed to come from them.

Learning Together

Video Study and Discussion

To set the stage for viewing the video, ask group members to jot down in their books or journals what they believe defines their own individual identity. Then ask them to consider this question: what limitations are your life pictures placing on you? Ask group members to note during the video what Mike Slaughter says about the difference between identity and birthright and how we can discover our birthright.

Following the video, discuss how group members defined their identity. Ask for a show of hands in response to the following:

- How many define identity in terms of their family role (such as father, mother, daughter, son)?
- How many define identity in terms of their job or vocation?
- Who included a passion or strong interest as a part of their identity?
- Who listed religious affiliation or beliefs?

Now ask volunteers to say how Mike Slaughter defines identity. (We are children of God living under the kingship of

P37

Jesus Christ.) Note that most people probably think of identity in terms of what makes us unique; in contrast, Slaughter views birthright, not identity, as the unique factor that differentiates each of us. How does he say we discover our birthright?

Invite brief comments from participants about particular insights that struck them as they viewed the video.

Bible Study and Discussion

This session continues the story of Jacob in Genesis 28. Review with the group the reasons Jacob had to flee so far from home. Ask a group member to summarize briefly how Jacob deceitfully secured his father's blessing and the birthright that should have been his brother's.

Invite someone to read aloud Genesis 28:18. Recall for group members that in the study book and video segment Mike Slaughter points out that what Jacob saw at the top of the ladder (or staircase) was God. Slaughter urges us to ask ourselves what (or who) is at the top of our ladder, since he believes that our life dreams will be limited by the ceiling of our life pictures. Invite the group to picture their own personal ladder. Is God at the top, or is something else—such as a job, a vocational ambition, or even another person?

Now encourage the group to answer the question posed by Slaughter: what limitations are your life pictures placing on you?

Have someone read aloud verses 20-22, the remainder of the scriptural foundation for today's session. Keep in mind Mike Slaughter's warning that after a period of serious discernment about life mission, God's vision for one's life may be so expansive that we might be intimidated. Discuss:

- Have you, like Jacob, ever placed conditions on how you might respond to God, hesitating to embrace a step forward in your faith that seems a little too big? If so, consider sharing it with the group. How did your reservations get in the way of your response?

" Change the world purpose.'

- Mike Slaughter observes that Jacob's very name meant what most of us today would call "identity theft." Later (Genesis 32), God gives Jacob a new name: Israel, indicating that Jacob has wrestled with God as well as with humans such as his father-in-law, Laban, and his brother, Esau. Ask participants to name other character qualities they see in Jacob. Are there some qualities that initially seem negative that God perhaps saw differently?

Encourage participants to reflect on qualities in themselves that might seem to be negatives. Which of those qualities might God be calling us to transform through our life mission into positives?

P39

Mike Slaughter states that we can only discover our birthright through an intimate relationship with the Holy Spirit. Form two groups. Give one group a sheet headed "God the Father" and the other a sheet headed "God the Son (Jesus Christ)." Invite each group to use a marker to jot down what they know about that person of the Godhead. Have each group report what they recorded to the large group, and give each group an opportunity to add their own comments to the other group's sheet.

2:9-10

Have volunteers read aloud the passages from 1 Corinthians and Galatians about the workings of the Holy Spirit that Slaughter notes in the study book. As a large group, work on a third sheet headed "God the Holy Spirit," brainstorming qualities of the Spirit and how the Spirit works. Invite the group to respond to the following statement and question:

- God comes into our lives through the Spirit, which serves as the ladder that connects us and leads us in all things to come.
- How do we develop an intimate relationship with the Holy Spirit?

Gal 1:1-
2:1-2

Eph 4:11
Gen. 32

Book Study and Discussion

Mike Slaughter recounts that he was part of a group of pastors identified by a team of successful Christian business people as young church leaders who had been "called." The group met with executives from companies including Southwest Airlines, DreamWorks, and Harley-Davidson.

Discuss what Slaughter calls the theology of tattoos. If any group members have tattoos, invite them to tell what the tattoos represents for them. Are they simply ways to adorn their bodies, or are they symbols of what is at the top of their ladders? Distribute paper, pencils, and fine-lined black markers or pens. Ask group members to sketch out on the paper a "tattoo" that depicts what they believe is at the top of their ladders. Encourage them to be brutally honest in this exercise. If, in examining the way they live their lives, it is obvious that something or someone other than God is truly the highest priority, that priority should be the tattoo they depict.

After allowing some time for participants to work, ask volunteers to share their tattoos with the group. Discuss:

- If your tattoo indicates that something other than God is at the top of your ladder, evaluate what is there. Does it represent a passion or strongly held conviction that might provide clues to your God-purpose?
- Mike Slaughter gives examples of people who found their birthright in times of brokenness. Can you identify insights from your own experiences of brokenness that might point the way to your God-purpose?

Slaughter recounts how God came to him in a waking vision in which he was humbled by knowing more about a sedan than the Sudan. Similarly, an activity called "praying the news" can serve as an exercise in sharpening the group's sensitivity to waking visions where the Spirit might break in.

Form small groups and distribute copies of the front page and ad sections of a local newspaper, an Internet news site, or a news magazine such as *Time*. Invite each group to find a news article about a current local, national, or global crisis. Ask them to read the article aloud. Then have them find and read aloud one or more advertisements for electronic equipment, cars, or other consumer goods. Ask members to spend some time in silent reflection and meditation, inviting God's spirit to work in them. After some time in silence, invite volunteers to share any insights that came to mind. Point out that for many participants, insights may not be immediately evident, but may emerge in days and weeks to come as they work on developing their life mission statement.

Building Your Life Mission Statement: Part 2

Recall for the group that in Genesis 28:18, Jacob got up early in the morning, took the stone that he had put near his head, and set it up as a pillar to serve as a memorial stone. Mike Slaughter has put his life mission statement on a memorial stone, placing it where he can read it regularly. Ask volunteers to read aloud the three parts of Slaughter's life mission statement. Note that he says this statement differs from goals he develops that may change from year to year or as different life situations and circumstances arise. Ask participants to read over what Slaughter says about each part of his mission statement, and address together any questions that arise or clarifications needed.

Mike Slaughter's mentor recommended addressing three questions to begin the process of developing a life mission statement:

- Where do you see the greatest need around you in your neighborhood, your community, or your world?
- How can you meet that need?
- What gifts do you bring to further that mission?

For the first question, brainstorm with the group some of the greatest needs in your community, the nation, and the world. Discuss the following:

- How might you address a specific need you have identified?
- Slaughter believes that you don't discover your gifts and then serve; your gifts emerge out of your service. How do you respond to that?

Point out that Slaughter emphasizes the importance of tithing, as Jacob promised to do in Genesis 28:22. Encourage group members to consider how their giving of time and talents compares to a tithe. If they fall short, how might they begin to increase their commitments?

Wrapping Up

Closing Activity

Ask group members to begin grappling with answers to the three questions posed in the study book before the next session. They may want to continue the spiritual discipline of praying the news as a way of opening themselves to the moving of the Spirit, or they may simply incorporate the breath prayer "Come, Holy Spirit" into their time of devotion.

Practice using this breath prayer together. Invite participants to find a comfortable position for sitting, exhaling, and consciously breathing out distractions and worries, then breathing in deeply to fill themselves with peace. Invite them to say silently "Come" as they inhale, and "Holy Spirit" as they exhale. Repeat several times.

Encourage group members during the coming days to be consciously aware of the possibilities of waking visions.

Closing Prayer

Close with the prayer Mike Slaughter uses to end Session 2 in the study book. Because Slaughter addresses Father God and prays in the name of Jesus Christ his Son, you may want to augment the prayer by inviting the workings of the third person of the Trinity, the Holy Spirit, by adding, "Come, Holy Spirit" and pausing for a time of silence before saying amen.

God, I am so thankful that in spite of our failures and distractions, you don't quit on us. You continually call us to live the great purpose for which you created us. Lord, empower us as we risk daring to dream your dream. In Jesus' name. Amen.

3. Your Burning Bush

Planning the Session

Session Goals

As a result of conversations and activities connected with this session, group members should begin to:

- define the three life stages involved in embracing one's life purpose,
- identify which of the three life stages they are currently experiencing and the prayer that is emerging from that stage,
- discern whether they have experienced a burning bush event, and
- continue work to prepare for creating their life mission statement.

Biblical Foundation

There the angel of the LORD appeared to [Moses] in a flame of fire out of a bush; he looked, and the bush was blazing, yet it was not consumed. Then Moses said, "I must turn aside and look at this great sight, and see why the bush is not burned up."

(Exodus 3:2-3 NRSV)

Getting Started

Opening Prayer

God of the ages, by your Spirit, open our eyes and our hearts to the signs of your never-failing presence, and to that purpose for which you created us. Guide us as we seek to discern how our own pasts can shape the future. In the name of Jesus Christ we pray. Amen.

Opening Activity

As group members arrive, welcome them. Ask them to talk together in pairs about how they responded to the questions from last session. Before breaking into pairs, review the questions with them:

- Where do you see the greatest need around you in your neighborhood, your community, or your world?
- How can you meet that need?
- What gifts do you bring to further that mission?

After reviewing the questions, ask the group to form pairs and discuss:

- What were the sticking points they encountered in addressing the questions? Did they find themselves overwhelmed when considering how they might meet the needs they identified?
- If, as Mike Slaughter contends, we discover our gifts as we serve, how did they answer the last question?

Depending on the ages of your group, participants may or may not already have some idea of the gifts they could bring to bear. Remind them that even if they know some of their gifts, there may be other, undiscovered gifts that could be revealed in discussion and in service.

Learning Together

Video Study and Discussion

Before viewing the video segment, designate the corners of your space with one of the following: Silent Generation (born around 1925–1945); Boomers (around 1946–1964); Gen X (around 1965–1984); Millennials (around 1985–early 2000s). Ask participants to go to the corner that matches their generation. (If you have a group member born before 1925, that person can remain seated in the center of the room as a representative of the GI Generation.) Tell the group that generational theory has been bandied about quite a bit in the past few years to explain how people of a certain age group are shaped by common experiences. Ask each group to discuss together what they think is an experience our society went through that had a profound impact on everyone of their age cohort—for example, for members of the Silent Generation, it might be the bombing of Pearl Harbor. If your group members are all a part of one generational cohort who have grown up in the United States, they have all been shaped to some degree by the same common national experiences.

Tell the group that, in contrast to generational theory, the three life stages that Mike Slaughter introduces in the video are not dependent on a person's age. A twenty-year-old may be well on the way to discovering his or her life purpose, while an eighty-year-old may just be beginning the process. These life stages are also intensely personal experiences. Invite the group to be alert to what is being said in the segment about these life stages.

Look, Listen Life
p-55 Stages

Following the video, invite the group to name the three life stages, as well as the three prayers Mike Slaughter says are characteristic of each stage. Tell the group that you will delve more deeply into the stages later in the session. For now, invite participants to begin to ask the questions of themselves:

- Which life stage do I seem to be experiencing?
- What is my recurring prayer to God?
- Have I experienced a burning bush moment?

Bible Study and Discussion

Ask group members to scan Exodus 2 quickly to refresh their memories about Moses from his birth to the point where today's Scripture takes up the story. Invite a volunteer or two briefly to summarize. Remind the group that although Moses was a Hebrew, he had been raised in Egyptian court and was thoroughly Egyptianized in terms of custom and dress. Indeed, after he fled the scene of his crime in Exodus 2, the daughters of the priest of Midian reported to their father that an Egyptian had helped them.

Suggest to group members that they listen to today's Scripture as if they themselves were Moses. Invite them to find a comfortable position for sitting and to close their eyes, imagining that they are tending flocks around the base of Mount Horeb. Read aloud Exodus 3:1-10.

Following the Scripture reading, ask for one word or a short phrase in response to each of the following: what did you see? hear? feel?

Book Study and Discussion

Mike Slaughter observes that all of us yearn to find the reason we were created: it is the ultimate hunger. He contends that many of us may not be able to name the hunger and may try to satisfy it with other things. Yet if we look for it, we can all have a burning bush experience.

Why were you created?

Invite the group to consider the three life stages introduced in the video segment and explained in more depth in the study book. As you explore these life stages, ask participants to keep in mind what stage they sense they are in at this time. Because many adults either have already experienced Stage 1, empire building, or are at present in that stage, consider this stage together. Invite group members to read over the information in the study book about Stage 1 and its three driving forces. Then form groups of three. Ask each small group to read Luke 4:1-13 to refresh their memories about the temptation of Jesus. In each small group, ask one person to consider appetite, one to consider approval, and one ambition. Then have them share in their small group, giving examples from their own experience or examples they have heard or observed of that driving force in action.

Reassemble the large group; then ask each small group to share one of the examples that emerged in their group. If some in the group feel that they are presently in Stage 1, invite them to complete these sentences in their books or journals: "God, bless me. I want to do your will and find your purpose for my life, and I'll do it eventually. But right now I'm busy. . ." Ask those who feel they are in Stage 2 to respond as they might have when they were experiencing that stage. Ask those who are willing to share what they wrote.

Mike Slaughter labels Stage 2 as disillusionment and observes that this stage is usually initiated by a crisis, often by what we might call a midlife crisis. In the large group, invite group members who believe they are experiencing or have experienced that stage to respond in writing in their books or journals to the following:

God, I thought that _____ would fulfill my life, but I was wrong. Now I'm confronted by this crisis of _____. God, save me!

After allowing some time for writing, ask for volunteers who are willing to share what they wrote with others in the large group.

Invite group members who have self-identified as still being in Stage 1 to discuss the following:

- What are the aspects of your life that are consuming your time and energy? (Encourage them to refer to the previous exercise.); and
- What if I lose the things that presently seem to be the center of my life, or if those things prove to be less fulfilling than I had hoped?

Discuss the following:

- Mike Slaughter believes that moments of crisis are the points at which we are most receptive to a burning bush. What have you experienced as a result of crisis?

Book Study Through the Lens of the Bible

To discuss Stage 3, invite participants to revisit Moses' encounter with God in the burning bush. Slaughter observes that a defining event that leads to your life purpose, like Moses' burning bush, creates a fire that will not be extinguished. Slaughter defines a burning bush moment as a time when you hear God's voice in a personal way so that you can know your purpose. Ask the group to respond to this question:

- Can you identify an experience similar to Moses', when you felt a definite call from God?

Have group members who responded in the affirmative form a group to discuss the following:

- How did you experience God's voice? If you sensed an interior voice, how did it express itself? If it came through a messenger, who was the messenger?
- How did you respond to the voice? Did you turn away, like Moses?

- Was your burning bush experience tied to your previous life experiences in some way? If so, how?

Ask group members who cannot identify a burning bush experience to form a group to discuss the following:

- Can you identify one or more experiences from your past that have had an impact on your life similar to the ones Mike Slaughter described from the lives of Martin Luther King Jr. or Oskar Schindler? If there is no single experience, can you name smaller painful experiences that have shaped you in some way?
- If there has been no burning bush, what about persistent embers through God that may be speaking with a quieter yet still pervasive message?

Point out to this group that Slaughter affirms it is okay to be unsure of God's dream for you or to feel stuck. In that case, the prayer "God, save me" can be lifted up without reservation, asking God to show you what God intends for your life.

Slaughter observes that a true God-purpose will not burn you up or burn you out and that your life mission will always be connected to God's redemptive purpose, not your own self-interest. In the large group, discuss:

- Can you identify aspects of your work or family life, volunteer work, or community service activities that are either consuming you or burning you out? Why do you think this is so?
- If so, what does this say to you about these activities? What can you do to help the situation?

Invite the group to consider in silence the following questions posed by Mike Slaughter at the end of the chapter:

- Which of these three life stages am I in right now?

- What am I praying? Is it God bless me, God save me, or God use me?
- Have I seen a burning bush?
- Do I feel I have heard from God about my BHAG?

Building Your Life Mission Statement: Part 3

Call the group's attention to the questions posed in "Building Your Life Mission Statement: Part 3." The questions are:

- What struggles in your life have you had to overcome? How have those struggles defined you?
- God can use all things to strengthen his kingdom, and we are called to do the same. How can you share the lessons learned from your struggles?
- How have those lessons helped you in the past, and how might God use them to shape your future?

Tell participants that whether or not they believe they have already experienced a burning bush encounter, it can be helpful to ponder these questions in order to see how past experiences have influenced where they are now. Invite participants to talk in pairs about the first question, about the struggles they have endured and how those struggles have defined them.

Wrapping Up

Closing Activity

Tell the group that they are now at the midpoint of this study. Call the group's attention once again to the sheet on which you recorded Mike Slaughter's three purposes for writing the study book:

- to wake up those in the study to the God-dream inside,
- to help participants develop a life mission statement, and

- to challenge participants to commit fully to the God-directed life mission they create.

One hopes the first purpose, that of being waked up to the God-purpose inside each person, is bearing fruit in the group members. Group members should also be well along the way in the process of developing a life mission statement. As you move into the final three sessions, ask participants to begin considering whether and how they are willing to commit fully to that mission, whatever it may be.

Closing Prayer

Ask the partners from today's exercise to take a few moments to pray for each other, asking God's Spirit to move and stir up that person so that the lessons from his or her struggles might be revealed and the way forward with those learnings might become clear.

4. LOSE YOUR BIG BUTS

Planning the Session

Session Goals
As a result of conversations and activities connected with this session, group members should begin to:

- identify the "big buts," the tightly held excuses prohibiting them from living God's dream for them;
- name the self-limiting beliefs held by others that are holding them back; and
- continue taking steps toward developing a life mission statement.

Special Preparation
- prepare cards—one set for every three participants or so—on which you have printed the following: United Theological Seminary; the Wright Dunbar Visitor Center cycle shop; Carillon Historical Park, home of the Wright Brothers Aviation Center; circuit rider; bicycles; and helicopter toy. These will be used in a session activity.

- (optional) If possible before the session, plan to view the YouTube video about Nick Vujicic and Rick Warren to which Mike Slaughter refers in the study book (http://www.oprah.com/oprahs-lifeclass/How-Nick-Vujicic-Triumphed-Against-All-Odds-Video). If you'd like the group to view it, you could use a laptop and video projector, or participants could view it on their smartphones.

Biblical Foundation

But Moses said to God, "Who am I to go to Pharaoh and to bring the Israelites out of Egypt?...If I now come to the Israelites and say to them, 'The God of your ancestors has sent me to you,' they are going to ask me, 'What's this God's name?' What am I supposed to say to them?...But what if they don't believe me or pay attention to me? They might say to me, 'The LORD didn't appear to you!' ...My Lord, I've never been able to speak well, not yesterday, not the day before, and certainly not now since you've been talking to your servant. I have a slow mouth and a thick tongue."

(Exodus 3:11, 13; 4:1, 10)

Getting Started

Opening Prayer

Remind the group that in the last session, Mike Slaughter offered the assurance that if we do not yet know our God-purpose, that is an okay place to be. Invite group members to pray with you, using the following:

Gracious God, there are those among us who are uncertain what your special purpose is for their lives. Together, we pray, God: save us. We don't know what you want us to do, but we are yours without reservation. Just show us!

There are others here, O God, who have experienced a burning bush pointing the way to their God-purpose. Together, we pray, God: use us. We are yours and you are ours.

And now guide us as we further seek to discern what you would have us do. In the name of Jesus Christ. Amen.

Opening Activity

As group members arrive, welcome them. Ask them to form pairs or groups of three and talk about their responses to the second question from last week's session:

- God can use all things to strengthen the Kingdom, and we are called to do the same. How can you share the lessons learned from your struggles? *Karen's mom*

If participants so choose, they can briefly share the defining struggles they named in the first question:

- What struggles in your life have you had to overcome? How have those struggles defined you?

However, it's fine if the group decides they want only to talk about the lessons they believe they learned from those struggles.

Assemble the large group and invite participants to name briefly the struggles they discussed in the smaller groups. List the struggles at the front of the class under the title "Lessons Learned." Suggest that group members may want to record this list in their journals, so that insights of others can shed further light as they continue to develop their life mission statement.

Learning Together

Video Study and Discussion

Before viewing the video segment, recall for group members that Mike Slaughter has used the life story of the Wright brothers as a way to introduce and frame each video. Distribute to pairs or small groups the cards on which you have printed the settings for the three previous videos (United Theological Seminary, the Wright Dunbar Visitor Center cycle shop, and the Carillon Historical Park, home of the Wright Brothers Aviation Center). Also give them cards on which you have printed the following: circuit rider, bicycles, and helicopter toy. Invite the small groups to match the video setting with the appropriate "object lesson" item.

Then reassemble the large group and ask for volunteers to explain the point Slaughter was making to introduce each previous video. (Video 1: Seminary setting; the brothers' father was a circuit rider preacher who taught them that they were created in God's image. Video 2: Cycle shop; while repairing bicycles was the brothers' day job, they had a much bigger picture in mind. Video 3: Aviation center; the gift of a helicopter-like toy sparked an interest.)

Tell group members that today's video is set in a somewhat surprising setting: a cemetery. As they watch, ask them to imagine why Slaughter would choose such a setting. Then watch the video.

Afterward, ask volunteers to explain the choice of a cemetery for the setting for this video. Then suggest that they jot down their birthdates in their journals, followed by a dash. Obviously they cannot know the dates of their deaths, but they do know that they have a limited time between the dash and the addition of that final date on a grave marker. Encourage them to keep this fact in mind as they explore the excuses we hold onto and the self-limiting beliefs we all tend to internalize that come from inside and outside.

Book Study Through the Lens of the Bible

Review the story of Moses from last time, as described in Exodus 3:1-10. Do this by asking someone to state in one sentence the beginning of the account; then ask others to add one sentence each to the account. If there is a detail left out, the next person can back up and add it before going forward. Continue until you have reviewed the entire passage up through verse 10.

Ask two or three volunteers to read aloud Exodus 3:10–4:17. Refer the group to the paragraph in the study book under the heading "A Boatload of Buts." Invite group members to imagine being eighty years old and receiving a calling from God such as Moses received. Moses' response in this session's Scripture reading is to come up with a number of excuses, which Slaughter calls "big buts." Together, discuss the first "but," found in Exodus 3:11, using these questions:

READ Mike Slaughter observes that if you feel qualified for your life mission, then your mission probably is not big enough. What is your response to this?

- Should a life mission stretch and challenge you? To what degree? Do you think it's possible for God to call you to a life mission that truly is beyond your capabilities?

- How do you feel about God's promise to be with us always? In what ways is that a comfort for you?

Form three smaller groups to consider the other three "buts" in this passage. On three separate sheets, print Moses' excuses, and place these sheets on tables or on the wall at intervals around your space. Assign one excuse to each group as a beginning point. Invite them to read the portion of the chapter that addresses the assigned excuse and discuss it together. On the sheet, ask them to print relevant points from their discussion. Then ask them to formulate a question or two for the other two groups to consider.

After allowing a few minutes for groups to work, ask each group to move to a new excuse, read and discuss the material in the study book, and discuss and respond to the question posed by the first group. Again allow some time for discussion; then have groups move to the final excuse. Read and discuss the study book information, and respond to the question posed on the sheet.

Come together to debrief this exercise. Ask:

- Which of the excuses do you, personally, find the biggest challenge as you consider your life purpose?
- Are there other excuses you might make to avoid embracing a life mission to which God may be calling you?
- Slaughter, who writes that he is an introvert with a fear of public speaking, observes that when he is preaching, God's strength is revealed through Slaughter's weakness. He quotes Eugene Peterson as saying that incompetence may be the essential qualification.[1] What does Peterson mean? Do you agree or disagree, and why?

If possible, view the YouTube video about Nick Vujicic and Rick Warren to which Slaughter refers in the study book (http://www.oprah.com/oprahs-lifeclass/How-Nick-Vujicic-Triumphed-Against-All-Odds-Video). After watching the clip together, invite responses and comments from the group.

Mike Slaughter says that many of us give our lives to Christ but keep the same old thoughts. In order for God to bring about what you were created to do, there must be a renewing of your mind. Discuss:

- What thoughts, attitudes, or habits might you need to let go of in order to embrace the life mission God intends for you?
- What might need to be renewed or transformed?

Slaughter notes that sometimes we claim negative beliefs that are laid on us by others, limiting our goals and creating paralyzing fears. Invite a volunteer to read aloud Numbers 13:17-20, 27-33.

Mike Slaughter states that he has a rule: speak faith when you feel futility. What does he mean? Can you recall a time when the negativity of others got in the way of accomplishing a goal?

Building Your Life Mission Statement: Part 4

Slaughter notes that there is a big difference between an obstacle and an excuse. Encourage group members to make note of obstacles they must work through, over, or around, perhaps listing them in their books or journals and then noting steps they can take to deal with them. Invite the group to read over the questions under "Building Your Life Mission Statement: Part 4."

E Noot Chapter

- What tightly held excuses prohibit you from living God's dream for you?
- Excuses aren't always something we come up with on our own. Sometimes we claim self-limiting beliefs assigned to us by others. From what self-limiting beliefs do you need to break free?
- Becoming clear about your life mission statement means chopping away at excuses to follow the purpose God has for you. Take some time and write a prayer asking God to remove your excuses. List your excuses in the prayer.

Ask group members to identify excuses and self-limiting beliefs from others that prohibit them from living God's dream. Allow some time for group members to write a prayer asking God to remove their excuses, listing them as Slaughter suggests.

Wrapping Up

Closing Activity

Recall for the group that the setting of this week's video was the cemetery where the Wright brothers are interred. Slaughter used this setting to make the point that all of us will die; we have a limited time to identify God's purpose for us and to live out our life mission to the best of our ability.

Remind the group that Jacob marked the place where he encountered God with a memorial stone, to serve as a reminder to others that the spot represented holy ground. A person's grave marker is a different kind of memorial stone, one that records a person's life span and serves as a reminder of a life lived. While the practice is less common than it once was, some people still include a short statement called an epitaph, intended to convey the sum of a person's life in a very few words.

Invite group members to think about an epitaph during the coming week. They might be shortened versions of the life mission statements they are working on. They could be similar to what businessman Ken Blanchard calls an elevator speech.[2] What words will sum up the lives they are leading?

END OF Construction Thankyou for your [Partner?]

Closing Prayer

Tell the group that you will close with a prayer in which they can ask God to remove their excuses and self-limiting beliefs assigned by others. Explain that in two places you will provide a few moments of silence in which they can consider these things. Then offer the following prayer:

Loving God, we desire to know what your purpose is for our *lives. We long to embrace that purpose and to live our lives in such a way as to fulfill what you would have us do. But so many things get in the way. We invent excuses that block us, leaving us unable to live the vision of the abundant life you intend. Hear us now as we ask that you remove all these excuses, and others that may become clear to us.* [Allow a time of silence for group members to lift up their excuses to God.]

At times, O God, we adopt the limitations others see in us instead of embracing the image of wholeness that you intend. Hear us now as we let go of perceptions that limit us and false portraits that block us from your desires for our lives. [Allow a time of silence for group members to lift up self-limitations.]

Renew our minds and our whole being. In the name of Jesus Christ. Amen.

5. WHAT IS IN YOUR HAND?

Planning the Session

Session Goals

As a result of conversations and activities connected with this session, group members should begin to:

- affirm that in God they already have everything they need to accomplish the mission they were created for,
- name some of the gifts and talents that are in their hands using three key questions, and
- take further steps toward developing a life mission statement.

Special Preparation

You will need several slips of paper for each participant, as well as a bowl or basket.

Biblical Foundation

The LORD's messenger appeared to him and said, "The LORD is with you, mighty warrior."

(Judges 6:12)

The LORD said to him, "What's that in your hand?" Moses replied. "A shepherd's rod." The LORD said, "Throw it down on the ground." So Moses threw it on the ground, and it turned into a snake. Moses jumped back from it. Then the LORD said to Moses, "Reach out and grab the snake by the tail." So Moses reached out and grabbed it, and it turned back into a rod in his hand. "Do this so that they will believe that the LORD, the God of their ancestors, Abraham's God, Isaac's God, and Jacob's God has in fact appeared to you."

(Exodus 4:2-5)

Getting Started

Opening Prayer

Ask one or two volunteers to offer the prayers they composed in response to the third part of their homework after last session: *Would someone share their prayer*

- Becoming clear about your life mission statement means chopping away at excuses to follow the purpose God has for you. Take some time and write a prayer asking God to remove your excuses. List your excuses in the prayer.

What are some of our excuses?

The volunteers can name the excuses they included in their prayer, or they can provide an interval of silence so that group members can lift up their own excuses silently to God. Close the time of prayer by invoking the Spirit's presence as the group explores the gifts and skills they bring to their emerging life mission statements.

Opening Activity

Welcome arriving group members, and invite them to form small groups. Suggest that the groups read Judges 6:1-6 and quickly formulate a job description for the kind of leader the Israelites needed in order to confront the Midianites. Tell them to make it brief; it should be the kind of description one might find in an ad in the newspaper or on the Internet.

In the large group, share the job descriptions that the smaller groups wrote. Ask a volunteer to read aloud Judges 6:11-16. Discuss:

- What kind of "mighty warrior" did God choose to commission?
- On the face of it, did Gideon possess any of the qualifications needed to do the job?

Ask group members to discuss Gideon's excuses and compare them with their own excuses. Mike Slaughter observes that Gideon couldn't get past his perceptions of the limitations he saw in himself because he was looking through human eyes, not God's eyes.

Ask someone to read aloud verses 33-35. Ask: what made the difference in Gideon's ability to respond?

As you continue forward in this session, encourage participants to invite the Holy Spirit to give them a new vision of their own possibilities. *Still Gideon questioned God. Test: Fleece - wet Fleece Not wet*

Learning Together

Video Study and Discussion

Before viewing today's video, recall with the group that each previous video had as its setting a place significant to the story of the Wright brothers. Today's video takes place in Hawthorn Hill, the home that Orville Wright built and lived in with his father and sister. Invite the group, when viewing the video, to watch for the question "what's in your hand?" as well as the three key questions Mike Slaughter poses that will help identify what's in your hand.

Following the viewing, call the group's attention to Mike Slaughter's statement that, in God, you already have everything you need to accomplish the mission you were created for. Ask someone to explain the analogy of the seed that Slaughter uses in the video. To extend the analogy further, discuss the following:

- If we are like a seed in which the genetic code to grow is already present, how does the Holy Spirit function to awaken that potential within us?
- What aspects or situations can you name that might prevent that potential from ever developing?

Ask the group to name the three key questions that will help identify the gifts and talents they are supposed to use in their life mission. (What are the gifts of my head? What are the gifts of my hands? What is the passion of my heart?) Tell them that you will discuss these questions in more depth later in the session.

Ask group members to explain or speculate why this segment was set in Hawthorn Hill. As the session continues, invite them to reflect on the fact that the Wright brothers continued to use their skills to innovate, beyond that major innovation of flight. Once we recognize and unleash our gifts and talents, the potential for using them continues as we seek our God-purpose.

Bible Study and Discussion

Invite a volunteer to read aloud Exodus 4:1-17. From the information in the video and the study book, ask group members to name some of the ways in which shepherds use their staffs. Then form three small groups or pairs and assign one of the following passages to each: Exodus 7:14-25; Exodus 14;

Exodus 17:1-7. Ask each group to describe how Moses used the staff in these passages, then lead a discussion using the following questions:

- Mike Slaughter observes that there was no way Moses the shepherd could have envisioned using his staff in such powerful ways. He names the computer as an ordinary tool of his own that has potential to be used for God's purposes. What ordinary tools are at your disposal that might have power you have not imagined?
- Slaughter observes that God often demonstrates the transforming power of simple tools to fulfill God's purposes, but one's collective life experience can be an equally powerful tool. Name some ways in which Moses' life experience growing up in Pharaoh's household might have been useful.
- Moses, says Slaughter, could have considered his life a failure. He experienced an abrupt descent from the position of power and influence in Pharaoh's household to that of a lowly shepherd. If you experienced a failure you were later able to use or learn from, and if you feel comfortable sharing it with the group, talk about it briefly.
- Name some other persons from the Bible who were able to fulfill expansive God-purposes, despite having flaws that would seem to limit their potential.

Again, what are the 3 questions?

Building Your Life Mission Statement: Part 5

From the video and the study book, ask group members to name the three key questions Mike Slaughter suggests will help them identify their gifts and talents. (What are the gifts of my head? What are the gifts of my hands? What is the passion of my heart?) List these questions in front of the class where they can refer to it. Then invite volunteers to summarize briefly some of the examples Slaughter gives from his own life of gifts of the head and hands and passion of his heart.

Encourage group members to think about these three questions in the same way they would a self-analysis prior to writing up a résumé, except that this résumé is not for a new job but for a lifelong mission. Allow several minutes for group members to think about how to answer each question about themselves and to record their responses on three separate sheets of paper, one for each question.

Also encourage the group not to think too narrowly—for example, limiting their lists to "book knowledge" as they think about what they know. Reviewing the examples Slaughter includes in the study book will help to point them in the right direction.

Dividing the group into pairs or smaller groups of no more than three persons (preferably those who know each other fairly well), invite participants to take each question in turn and pass their papers to another person to read. That person can then comment or add to the sheet additional gifts the original author may not have listed.

When everyone has had a chance to read and comment on the responses about gifts and talents, take a few moments to debrief in the large group. Discuss:

- How did it feel to put your gifts and talents in writing?
- What was it like to get responses from one or two other persons?

Point out for group members that this process of identifying gifts and talents should not end with one class exercise or with class members who may or may not know them well. Encourage them to identify two or three people who do know them very well, such as a family member, a co-worker, and a close friend. Before the next session, they should ask these persons to read over their sheets and make comments or suggestions of gifts and talents that may not have seemed obvious to the person making the list.

Also encourage group members to consider ~~their~~ *your* own life experience—not just professional or vocational experience, but also events or experiences in ~~their~~ *your* lives that have given ~~them~~ *you* a different perspective than those of other people. They should include failures and hard times they have endured and from which they emerged with new learnings as well as more successful experiences.

Mike Slaughter points out that, at God's direction, Moses threw down his staff, taking a bold and definitive action. Ask:

- What happens when it seems too risky or costly to offer a gift to God?
- What does Slaughter mean when he says that we can't think our way into a new way of acting; we have to act our way into a new way of thinking? Do you agree or disagree? Why?

Wrapping Up

Closing Activity

Mike Slaughter observes that many of us are living in spiritual poverty, when just beneath the surface, we have the power of the Holy Spirit and an array of gifts just waiting to be activated. Encourage class members to continue the exercise at home of having people close to them read and comment on their lists of gifts and talents.

Also ask participants to keep in mind Slaughter's account of having his master's degree students meet in the original Ginghamsburg church building, where they consider what they might have thought the God-potential was for that small country church. In the coming days, invite your group members to be alert to places where the Holy Spirit's power is desperately needed, trying to view these places through God's eyes, or at least through the eyes of one who is seeking to know God's purpose.

Distribute one or more slips of paper to group members. Invite them to write on the slips some of the gifts and talents they have identified in this session that they can offer to God during the closing prayer. If there are persons in the group who are still uncertain about the gifts and talents they have, assure them that it's okay. In that case, they may want to write on a paper slip an indication of their willingness to be open to the work of the Holy Spirit in their lives, in moving toward greater discernment.

Closing Prayer

Pray the following, or a prayer of your own choosing.

Heavenly Father

Holy One, open us to the work of your Holy Spirit within us as we seek to discern what gifts and talents we can offer to serve your purposes. Some of us are ready to offer boldly what gifts we have to your service. Some of us are seeking to discern our gifts and talents and life experiences that can best further your mission.

All of these we offer now, trusting that your Spirit is with us always. [Invite group members to put their slips of paper in a basket or bowl.]

In the name of Jesus Christ your Son we pray. Amen.

6. PERSEVERANCE

Planning the Session

Session Goals

As a result of conversations and activities connected with this session, group members should:

- name and affirm how perseverance plays a key role in a sustaining life mission,
- complete a draft of their own life mission statement, and
- celebrate and give thanks for God's never-ending presence as they seek to live into a life mission that furthers God's purposes for the world.

Special Preparation

For the opening activity and prayer, download images of mountains from the Internet to project, or use a YouTube clip. One possibility is "The Mountain" at http://www.youtube .com/watch?v=Rk6_hdRtJOE. Alternatively, you may want to print out several pictures of mountains that you can display.

Biblical Foundation

Then Moses climbed Mount Nebo from the plains of Moab to the top of Pisgah, across from Jericho. There the LORD showed him the whole land.... Then the LORD said to him. "This is the land I promised on oath to Abraham, Isaac and Jacob when I said, 'I will give it to your descendants.' I have let you see it with your eyes, but you will not cross over into it." And Moses the servant of the LORD died there in Moab, as the LORD had said. He buried him in Moab, in the valley opposite Beth Peor, but to this day no one knows where his grave is. Moses was a hundred and twenty years old when he died, yet his eyes were not weak nor his strength gone.

(Deuteronomy 34:1, 4-7 NIV)

Getting Started

Opening Activity and Prayer

If you have been able to obtain a slide of mountains or a YouTube clip to project with a video projector, have it playing when group members arrive. Invite them to come in quietly and sit in silence until everyone else has arrived. Continue to project images or the video for a few minutes. Then remind them that mountains in Scripture usually signify a place to get a clearer vision. As the study book tells us, Moses received his first vision, that of the burning bush, at Mount Horeb. His final vision, recounted in today's Scripture passage, was at Mount Pisgah.

Ask participants to sit quietly as you play the clip or show the images again, praying that they can open themselves to the Holy Spirit in order to discern what their life mission will be and asking for the Spirit's guidance as they put their statements in draft form today. Close the time of prayer by praying:

Come, Holy Spirit, and open our eyes today. Give us clarity as to what God's dream is for each of us. In the name of Jesus Christ we pray. Amen.

Learning Together

Video Study and Discussion $Show$
DVD

This final video is set at Huffman Prairie Flying Field, where the Wright brothers developed the world's first practical aircraft in 1905, two years after their successful first mechanical flight. Invite the group to watch and see what Mike Slaughter has to say about forward vision and future focus, perseverance, and legacy.

Following the video, invite comments and observations, including what the segment says about legacy and the other forward-focused concepts. Then ask group members to consider the key questions posed near the end of the video:

- Where in your life do you need to go back and try again?
- Have you given everything you can?

Encourage group members to record these questions in their books or journals. In order to keep a future vision in sight, it may be necessary for them to take an inventory of how they have lived their lives and where they may need to "rewind" and revisit past experiences.

Bible Study and Discussion

Mike Slaughter recounts in the study book that Moses experienced a myriad of setbacks and frustrations. Invite the group to recall and name some of those setbacks, beginning with Moses' encounter with the Egyptian beating the Hebrew slave. List these setbacks for the class.

Invite a volunteer to read aloud Deuteronomy 34:1-7. Discuss the following:

- What does the Scripture mean when it says Moses was 120 years old when he died, yet his eyes were not weak nor his strength gone?

- Slaughter tells us that Moses was successful because he still had a sustaining vision. What would you say that vision was?
- Imagine being Moses and looking back on his life, reviewing the obstacles and difficulties he had to overcome. Now imagine looking forward across the land, which the Lord had promised to the people, yet hearing that Moses himself would not enter the land. How would you have responded had you been Moses?
- Slaughter observes that what our lives come down to is one word: *legacy*. What was Moses' legacy to his descendants? How did he ensure that the vision would be sustained after he was gone?

Book Study and Discussion

On paper or a board, print the following quotations:

- "Saints are sinners who kept on going." —Robert Louis Stephenson[1]
- "It's not that I'm smart, it's just that I stay at problems longer." —Albert Einstein[2]

Note that these quotations express the perseverance of people who had a vision for their lives. Slaughter names others who overcame daunting obstacles to succeed—Beethoven, Ray Charles, Stevie Wonder, James Earl Jones, Franklin D. Roosevelt. Invite the group to name others they can think of who have persevered to achieve, either noteworthy and famous people or people they have known. Discuss the following:

- Mike Slaughter writes: "Here is my philosophy of life: ready, fire, aim." He notes that we don't need to have all the resources at the outset of our mission to accomplish what God is calling us to do; the resources will be given at the appointed time. What is your response to this philosophy? Is this a foolhardy, shortsighted way to approach one's life mission, or a wise reliance on trusting God to provide? If you were to state your philosophy of life in just one phrase or sentence, what would it be?

• Slaughter uses the example of manna in the wilderness to make the point that successful people have a way of renewing and sustaining the vision so it does not burn out. He and his wife make a practice of going on visioning retreats every year. What resources does God make available to you so that you do not experience burnout? Which do you make use of on a regular basis?

Invite volunteers to describe the accounts in this chapter of when the Slaughters first went to Ginghamsburg and what transpired. Discuss the following:

• Slaughter envisioned a worshiping community of three thousand, as well as a faith community that was engaging its community and the world, but he encountered stiff resistance from the congregants in the small country church to which he was assigned. Ultimately that God-sized vision is being lived out, and Ginghamsburg Church continues to be guided by it. But suppose your God-sized mission does not seem to be coming to fruition? What tools can you bring to bear in order to persevere?

• Slaughter says the most important mission that all of us have is to make sure our children, grandchildren, and future generations will enter God's place of promise. How is that happening in Ginghamsburg? How is it happening, or how would you like to see it happening, in your own life?

Building Your Life Mission Statement: Part 6
Ask the group to turn in their study books to "Building Your Life Mission Statement: Part 6." Invite them to review

what they have written in their books or journals over the past five sessions in building their life mission statements.

Invite a volunteer to read aloud what Mike Slaughter urges us to remember as statements are being formulated. Also remind them of Slaughter's statement in Chapter 1 about how to determine if the life purpose you have discerned, and from which you will create your life mission statement, is truly from God: it will always honor God, bless other people, and bring you joy.

Ask someone to read Slaughter's three-part life mission statement, found in Chapter 2. Then have volunteers read aloud the examples of statements from members of Ginghamsburg Church at the beginning of the book chapter.

Distribute paper and pencils, and give group members several minutes to write a draft of their life mission statement. After allowing time for them to work, ask them to form pairs to share their statements. Ask group members to keep in mind that for some, these may be rough drafts or perhaps only glimmerings of ideas, while for others the statement may be nearly in final form. Invite group members to use the following process:

- Read the statement aloud to your partner.
- The partner responds by telling what he or she likes about the statement and asking for clarification where something is unclear.

Then have pairs form groups of four and again share their statements.

Slaughter encourages readers, once they have their draft of a life mission statement, to try writing an "elevator speech." Remind the group of the epitaphs they wrote in Session 4. Epitaphs are the same kind of short statement as an elevator speech, and can serve as a reminder that all the time we have is that between the dashes. A person's life mission statement could serve as a worthy epitaph.

Wrapping Up

Closing Activity

Invite a volunteer to read aloud Matthew 14:22-33, the account of Jesus walking on water and the response of Peter, someone whom Slaughter dubs his favorite screwup. After hearing the Scripture, read aloud these final paragraphs of the study book epilogue:

> Look back at the story of Peter and the boat. Jesus told him, "Come," and Peter responded.
>
> Jesus is the Son of God, resurrected from the grave. He is creator of the universe. He is Lord, with a capital *L*, which means he has absolute authority. When he beckons to you and says, "Come," how will you respond? "Tomorrow"? "Maybe some other time"?
>
> No! Get out of the boat! You will experience the miracle God made for you when you hear and obey what Jesus is saying in your life. That's the difference between a daydream and a God-dream. A God-dream happens when you put perspiration to inspiration.

Closing Prayer

Close with the prayer at the end of Chapter 6:

P 118

God, I am so thankful that you never let us go—in our distractions, in our false priorities, in our failures. Lord, clear our vision and renew our focus. Give us the courage to persevere. Amen.

Notes

1. Dreaming the Dream
1. Jim Collins, *Good to Great: Why Some Companies Make the Leap and Others Don't* (New York: HarperCollins, 2001), 190.

4. Lose Your Big Buts
1. Eugene H. Peterson, *Christ Plays in Ten Thousand Places: A Conversation in Spiritual Theology* (Grand Rapids: Eerdmans, 2005), 152.
2. Kenneth H. Blanchard and Spencer Johnson, *The One Minute Manager* (New York: William Morrow, 2003).

6. Perseverance
1. A quote often attributed to Robert Louis Stevenson, http://www.reference.com/motif/health/famous-quotes-about-never-giving-up.
2. http://www.getinspired365.com/20130314.

CPSIA information can be obtained at www.ICGtesting.com
Printed in the USA
LVOW09s0754280814

401029LV00004B/4/P